SCHOLASTIC

Math Games
to Master Basic Skills
TIME & MONEY

by Jennifer Overend Prior

NEW YORK • TORONTO • LONDON • AUCKLAND • SYDNEY
MEXICO CITY • NEW DELHI • HONG KONG • BUENOS AIRES

Teaching *Resources*

Edited by Immacula A. Rhodes
Cover design by Jason Robinson
Interior illustrations by Teresa Anderko
Interior design by Sydney Wright

ISBN-13: 978-0-439-55414-5
ISBN-10: 0-439-55414-4
Copyright © 2007 by Jennifer Overend Prior.
Published by Scholastic Inc.
All rights reserved.
Printed in the U.S.A.

2 3 4 5 6 7 8 9 10   40   14 13 12 11 10 09 08 07

Contents

Introduction

Math Games to Master Basic Skills: Time & Money provides a variety of engaging games to help students develop proficiency in working with time and money. Each game is designed with fun and function in mind: An entertaining theme or challenging format keeps students interested and motivated, while the focus on a specific skill reinforces and strengthens their understanding of time and money concepts.

The games in this book are designed to complement the curriculum and help students learn the important skills addressed in the National Council of Teachers of Mathematics (NCTM) standards. Games featuring time concepts give students opportunities to recognize and develop understanding of the attributes of time, including units and tools used to measure time. The money-related games encourage computational fluency by providing practice in adding and subtracting money values to solve problems. You can use these math games to increase students' mathematical knowledge and reinforce their use of a variety of strategies, methods, and tools as they explore and learn about time and money concepts. The games are ideal for students who need extra reinforcement and repeated practice to strengthen the basic skills they need to know.

To prepare students to use different strategies while playing the games, be sure to spend time helping them develop and use specific problem-solving strategies, such as the following:

Skill	Strategy
To skip-count	Teach students to group items by fives or tens and then practice skip-counting by these increments.
	Teach students to group minutes on the clock by five-minute and ten-minute increments and then skip-count to tell time or set time on the clock.
	Teach students the value of a nickel and dime (5¢ and 10¢) and then how to skip-count sets of each type of coin to find the value of the sets.
To use simple fractions	Teach students the relationship between $\frac{1}{2}$, $\frac{1}{4}$, and a whole unit.
	Teach students that one hour is divided into half-hour and quarter-hour increments. Use analog clocks to demonstrate the visual divisions and digital clocks to show the numerical divisions (such as 1:15, 1:30, and 1:45).
	Teach students the fractional relationship of a quarter and half-dollar to a dollar, how to group each type of coin to equal a dollar, and how to incrementally count coins in the sets up to a dollar value (for example, for a set of four quarters, they count 25¢, 50¢, 75¢, one dollar).
To count money	Teach students to count on from the greatest coin value to find the value of a combination of coins (for example, for a quarter, nickel, and two pennies, they start at 25¢ and count up by 5¢ and then 2¢).

As students solve time and money problems, ask them questions about how they reach their answers and encourage them to share, clarify, and compare the mathematical strategies they use. Susan Jo Russell, a mathematics educator at TERC (Technology Education Research Center), also stresses the importance of having students examine and discuss how and why their methods succeed or fail, and which strategies are most consistent and reliable (2000)*.

Each game in *Math Games to Master Basic Skills: Time & Money* includes a targeted skill and the recommended number of players, as well as a list of materials needed to play the game, directions on how to play, a variation that adds an interesting twist or challenge to the original game, and an answer key. There are a variety of ways you can use the games to meet the needs of your students. Store the games in your math center, then invite students to use them during center activities, free-choice time, before or after school, or when they have finished other tasks. You can also send the games home for students to play with family and friends. The variation for each game suggests an additional way to use elements of the game to build and reinforce students' skills and interest.

How to Prepare and Use the Games

Preparing the games for play is quick and easy. First, gather the materials listed for each game. Then copy the reproducible pages and color the game elements that feature art. Finally, laminate and cut out all the game pieces. Refer to the illustrations on the reproducible pages for instructions on how to assemble the game clock and any other game accessories, such as spinners and cubes.

In general, buttons work well as game markers. However, you might choose to substitute another type of item that is more readily available (such as paper clips, small construction paper squares, or plastic game chips) or relates to the game theme, such as small football-shaped erasers for Time on the Field or pig-shaped counters for Piggy Bank Play-Off.

For easy storage, keep all the pieces for each game in a large resealable plastic bag or laminated manila envelope. Be sure to include a copy of the game directions. Label the bag or envelope with the name of the game, the skill it reinforces, and the number of players.

To introduce the game, play it with students or assist them as they play. Also help them establish a method for determining the order in which players will take turns, such as by rolling a number cube and taking turns in numerical order or by taking turns in the order of their birthdays.

* **Source:**
  Russell, Susan Jo. "Developing Computational Fluency with Whole Numbers in the Elementary Grades." In Ferrucci, Beverly J. and Heid, M. Kathleen (eds). Millennium Focus Issue: Perspectives on Principles and Standards. *The New England Math Journal*. Volume 32, No. 2 (May, 2000): pp. 40–54.

o Fish

o Fish ········ · · · · · · · · · · · · · · · · · · ·

Materials

• Go Fish game cards (pages 7–9)

How to Play

1. One player shuffles the cards and deals five cards to each player. He or she places the stack of cards facedown on the table.

2. The first player checks his or her cards for analog and digital clocks that show the same time. If the player is holding one match (or more), he or she places it on the table. Then the player picks a card remaining in his or her hand, reads the time on it, and asks another player by name for a card with that time.

  ✳ If the named player is holding a card that shows that time, he or she gives it to the player who asked for it. The asking player then lays the new match on the table and takes another turn.

  ✳ If the named player does not have a card with the matching time, he or she says, "Go Fish." Then the asking player takes the top card on the stack, adds it to his or her hand, and the turn ends.

3. Players continue to take turns until a player uses all the cards in his or her hand or until no more matches can be made. When all the cards in the stack have been used, players continue by asking each other for time cards from their hands. If a named player does not have the matching card, the asking player's turn ends right then. The player with the most pairs of matching cards at the end of the game is the winner.

OBJECTIVE

To match time to the hour and half-hour on analog and digital clocks and be the player with the most cards at the end of the game

PLAYERS: 2–4

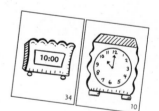

Variation

Each time a player makes a match, have him or her toss a penny onto the table. If the penny lands heads up, ask the player to add one-half hour to the time shown on his or her matching cards and then tell what the new time would be. If the penny lands tails up, have the player add an hour to the time shown on the matching cards.

Answer Key
The matching card pairs are:

1, 25	6, 30	11, 35	16, 40	21, 45
2, 26	7, 31	12, 36	17, 41	22, 46
3, 27	8, 32	13, 37	18, 42	23, 47
4, 28	9, 33	14, 38	19, 43	24, 48
5, 29	10, 34	15, 39	20, 44	

Go Fish Game Cards

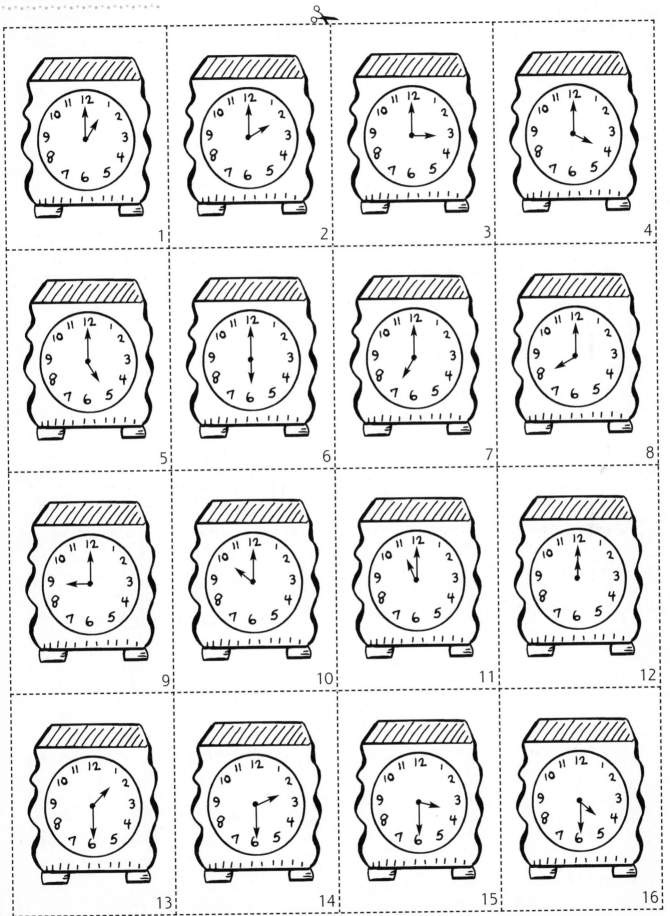

Go Fish Game Cards

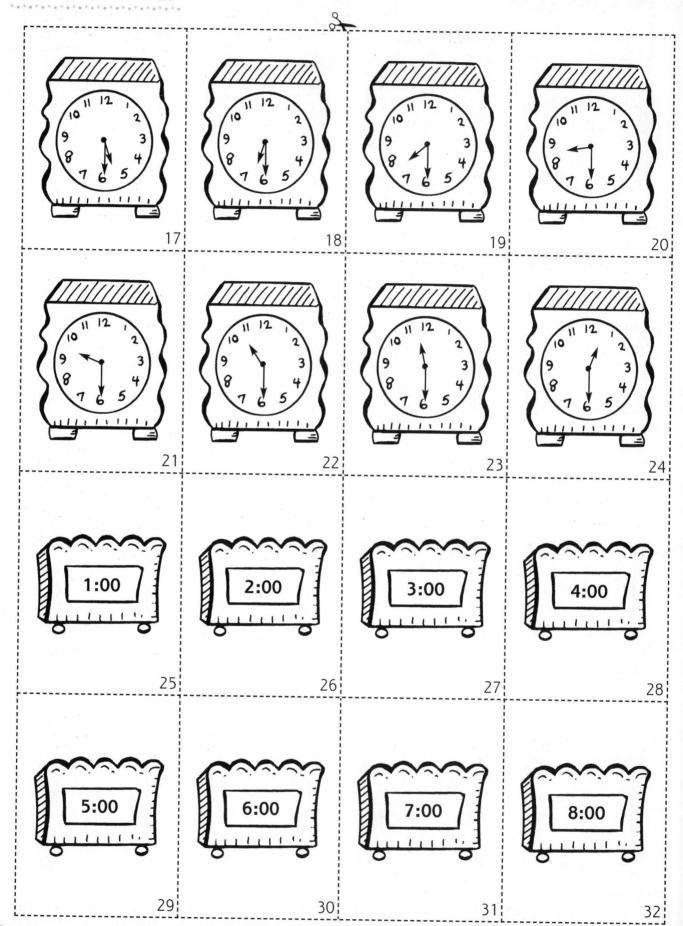

Math Games to Master Basic Skills: Time & Money Scholastic Teaching Resources

Go Fish Game Cards

Time-in-a-Row Bingo

Materials

- Time-in-a-Row Bingo game board for each player (page 11)
- Go Fish game cards 1–24 (pages 7–8)
- Time-in-a-Row Bingo game cards 49–64 (page 12)
- 9 buttons per player (for game markers)

How to Play

1. One player shuffles the cards and places the stack facedown on the table. Each player selects a game board.

2. The first player turns over the top card in the stack and names the time shown on the card. Then the player shows the card to all players. The players agree whether or not the first player named the correct time on the clock. If incorrect, they decide together what time is shown on the clock. Then they check their game boards for a digital clock showing the same time. If a player has a match, he or she covers that space with a marker. The game card is then placed in a separate stack and the turn ends.

3. Players continue to take turns reading the time on the top card in the stack. Each time a player finds a matching time on his or her game board, the player covers the space with a marker. The first player to cover three spaces in a row, going across, down, or diagonally, and to call out "Bingo!" wins the game. (Note: Players can check their answers by comparing the covered clocks on their game boards to the cards in the stack of called cards.)

Variation

Provide more opportunities for players to tell time by having them play until one player covers all the spaces on his or her game board.

OBJECTIVE

To match analog and digital times to the quarter-hour and be the first player to cover three spaces in a row on his or her game board

PLAYERS: 2–4

Answer Key
The numbers on the game boards below correspond to the number of the game card that matches the time shown on that space.

Game Board 1

53	10	50
19	60	23
12	15	4

Game Board 2

64	20	59
17	6	3
11	57	13

Game Board 3

58	16	9
54	18	51
7	22	2

Game Board 4

8	62	21
55	24	1
52	5	14

Time-in-a-Row Bingo Game Boards

Time-in-a-Row Bingo Cards

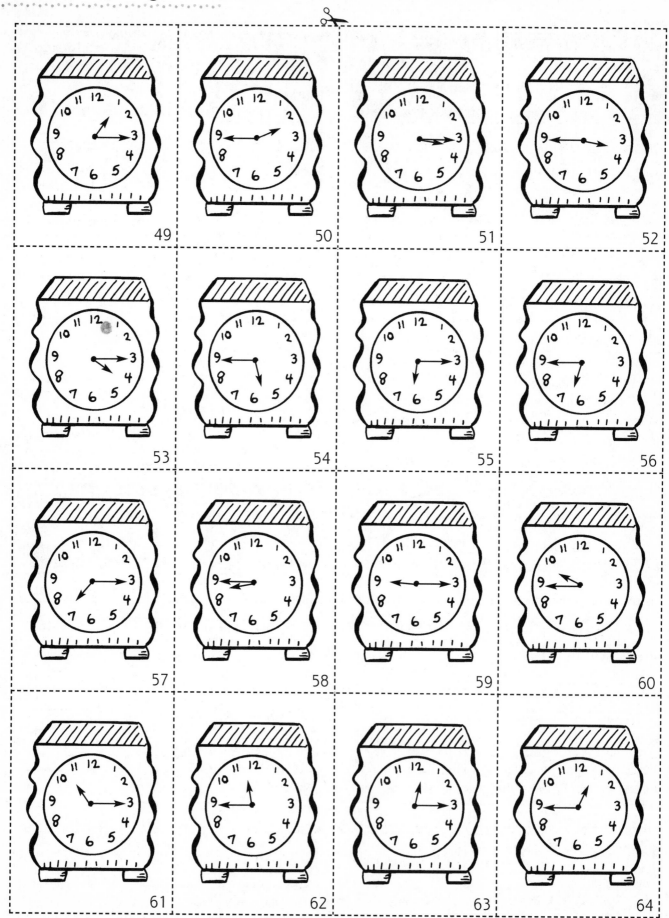

Tick-Tock-Toe! · · · · · · · · · · ·

Materials

- Tick-Tock-Toe! game board for each player (page 14)
- Tick-Tock-Toe! game cards (pages 14–15)
- Game Clock patterns (page 16)
- Brass fastener (for clock)
- 16 buttons per player (for game markers)

How to Play

1. One player shuffles the cards and places the stack facedown on the table. Each player selects a game board.

2. The first player removes the top card in the stack and, without looking at it, passes the card to the player to his or her left. That player reads the time phrase on the card. Then the first player sets the game clock to the named time. When finished, he or she takes the card and compares the time on the clock to the time shown on the card.

  ✳ If the player set the correct time on the clock, he or she covers a space on the game board that matches the type of clock shown on the card.

  ✳ If incorrect, the player puts the card on the bottom of the stack and the turn ends.

3. Players continue to take turns setting the clock and checking their work for correctness. The first player to cover four spaces in a row, going across, down, or diagonally, wins the game.

Variation

To reinforce computing the difference between two times, place the cards facedown on the table. To play, a player turns over two cards, reads the time on each clock, and then tells how much time difference there is between the two clocks. If the answer is correct, the player covers two spaces on his or her game board that match the two types of clocks on the cards. Players take turns until one player covers four spaces in a row. If all the cards have been used before the game ends, players shuffle the cards, place them facedown on the table, and continue play.

Answer Key
Answers are shown on the game cards.

> ## OBJECTIVE
>
> To set a clock to match specific time phrases and be the first player to cover four spaces in a row on his or her game board
>
> ## PLAYERS: 2–4

a quarter past 10

Tick-Tock-Toe!

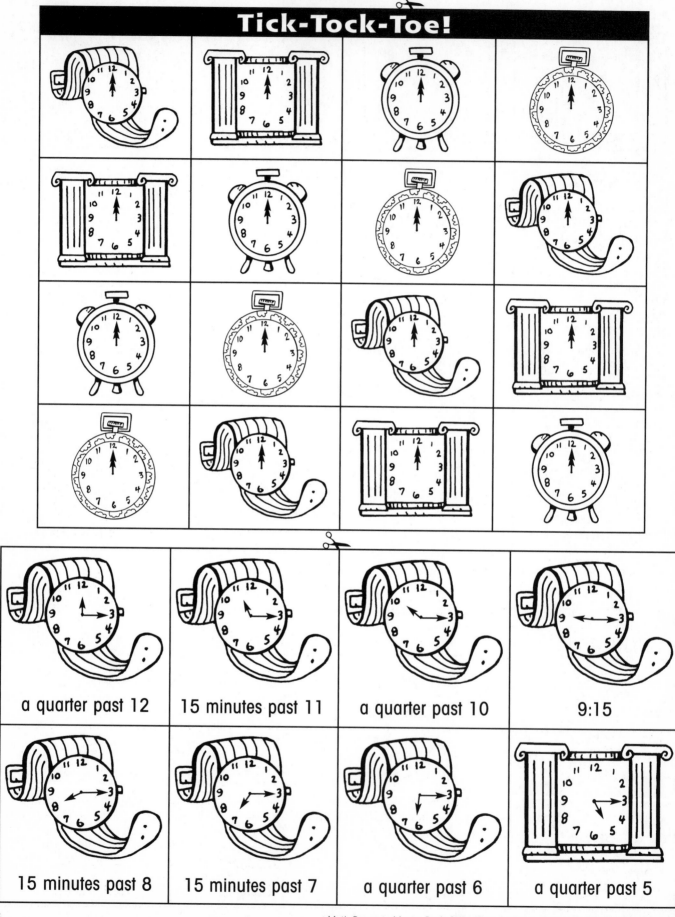

a quarter past 12	15 minutes past 11	a quarter past 10	9:15
15 minutes past 8	15 minutes past 7	a quarter past 6	a quarter past 5

Tick-Tock-Toe! Game Cards

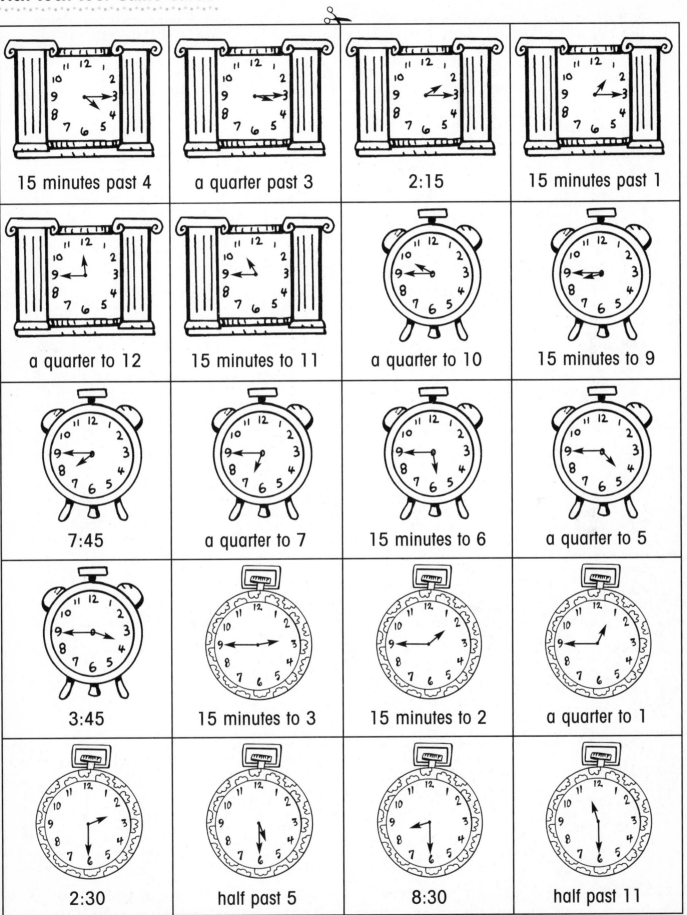

15 minutes past 4	a quarter past 3	2:15	15 minutes past 1
a quarter to 12	15 minutes to 11	a quarter to 10	15 minutes to 9
7:45	a quarter to 7	15 minutes to 6	a quarter to 5
3:45	15 minutes to 3	15 minutes to 2	a quarter to 1
2:30	half past 5	8:30	half past 11

Game Clock Pattern

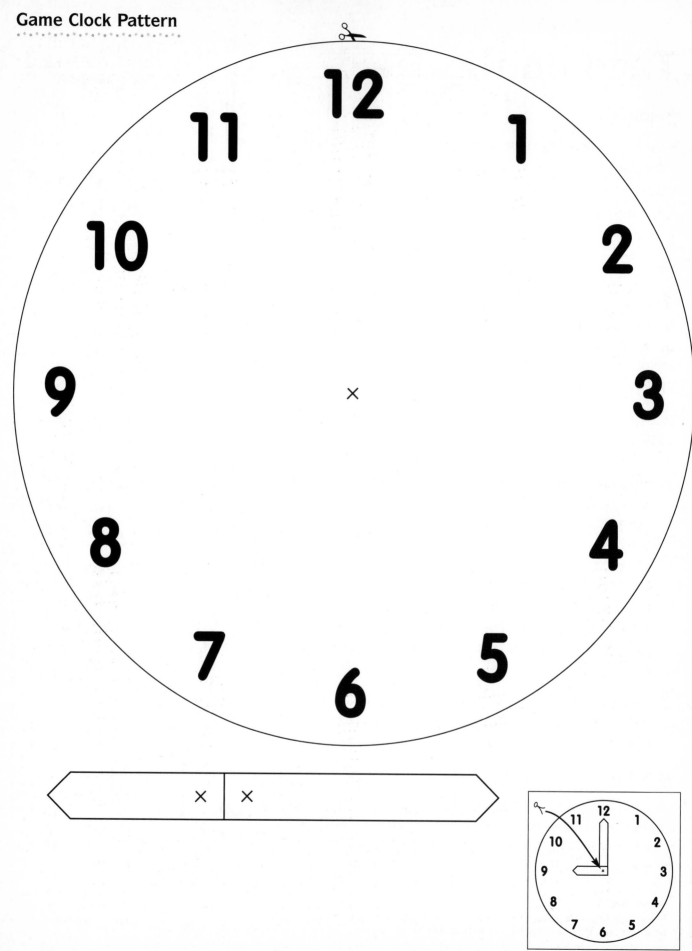

Math Games to Master Basic Skills: Time & Money Scholastic Teaching Resources

Time on the Field

Materials

- Time on the Field game board (page 18)
- Time on the Field game cards, 2 copies of each set (page 19)
- Game Clock patterns (page 16)
- Brass fastener (for clock)
- 1 button per player, each a different color (for game markers)

How to Play

1. One player shuffles the time cards and another player shuffles the field play cards. Each player places his or her stack facedown near the game board. Then each player selects one end of the game board. He or she places a marker on START at the 20 yard line on the opposite end of the game board.

2. The first player sets the game clock to 12:00. Then the player turns over the top card in the time card stack. He or she reads the card and follows the directions to set the clock.

 ✳ If the player sets the clock correctly, he or she takes the top card from the stack of field play cards. The player reads the card and moves his or her marker on the game board as directed. Then the turn ends and the player passes the clock, set at its new time, to the next player.

 ✳ If the player sets the clock incorrectly, the player returns the time card to the bottom of the stack, passes the clock to the next player, and the turn ends. The next player sets the clock to 12:00 before beginning his or her turn.

3. Players continue to take turns. The first player to move his or her game marker to the goal on his or her end of the game board wins the game.

Variation

To provide practice in adding and subtracting five-minute increments of time, replace the 0 in each number on the time cards with a 5. Then invite students to play the game using the new set of cards.

> **Answer Key**
> Answers will vary according to the directions shown on the time cards. Players should agree whether or not answers are correct.

OBJECTIVE

To add and subtract ten-minute increments of time and be the first player to move his or her marker to the goal line

PLAYERS: 2

17

0   **Goal!**   0

10   10

20   **Start**   20

30   30

40   40

50   50

40   40

30   30

20   **Start**   20

10   10

0   **Goal!**   0

Math Games to Master Basic Skills: Time & Money   Scholastic Teaching Resources

Time on the Field Game Cards

Time Cards

Add 10 minutes. Show the time.	Add 20 minutes. Show the time.	Add 30 minutes. Show the time.	Add 40 minutes. Show the time.
Add 50 minutes. Show the time.	Take away 10 minutes. Show the time.	Take away 20 minutes. Show the time.	Take away 30 minutes. Show the time.
Take away 40 minutes. Show the time.	Take away 50 minutes. Show the time.	Set the clock to 12:00. Show the time.	Set the clock to 6:30. Show the time.

Field Play Cards

Pass ball to teammate. Go ahead 10 yards.	Run ball down field. Go ahead 10 yards.	Catch pass. Go ahead 10 yards.	Catch pass. Go ahead 20 yards.
Time out. Do not move.	Time out. Do not move.	Halftime. Go to START.	Penalty. Go back 10 yards.
Penalty. Go back 10 yards.	Offside. Go back 10 yards.	Tackled! Go back 10 yards.	Tackled! Go back 20 yards.

Five-Minute Flowers

Materials

• Five-Minute Flowers game board for each player (page 21)
• Five-Minute Flowers game cards (page 21)

How to Play

1. One player shuffles the game cards and then places each card facedown on the table. Each player selects a game board.

2. The first player turns over one card, or flower petal. He or she tells the time shown on the clock. Then the player checks to see if that time is shown on his or her game board, or flower center.

* If the player finds a match, he or she places the petal next to the matching time on the flower center. Then the player takes another turn.

* If the player does not find a match, he or she returns the card facedown to the table and the turn ends.

3. Players continue to take turns. The first player to correctly match all six flower petals to his or her flower center wins the game.

Variation

Use only the petal cards to give students practice in sequencing times. To play, place six cards facedown in front of each player. Then, on a signal, each player turns over and sequences his or her cards from the earliest to latest times shown on the clocks. The first player to correctly sequence all of his or her cards wins the game.

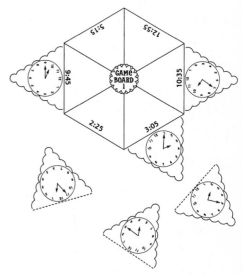

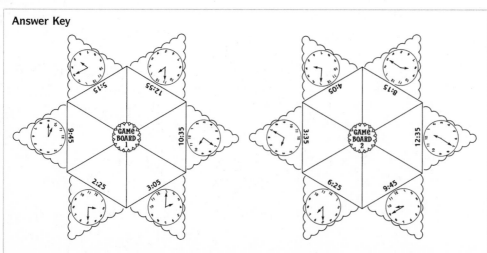

20

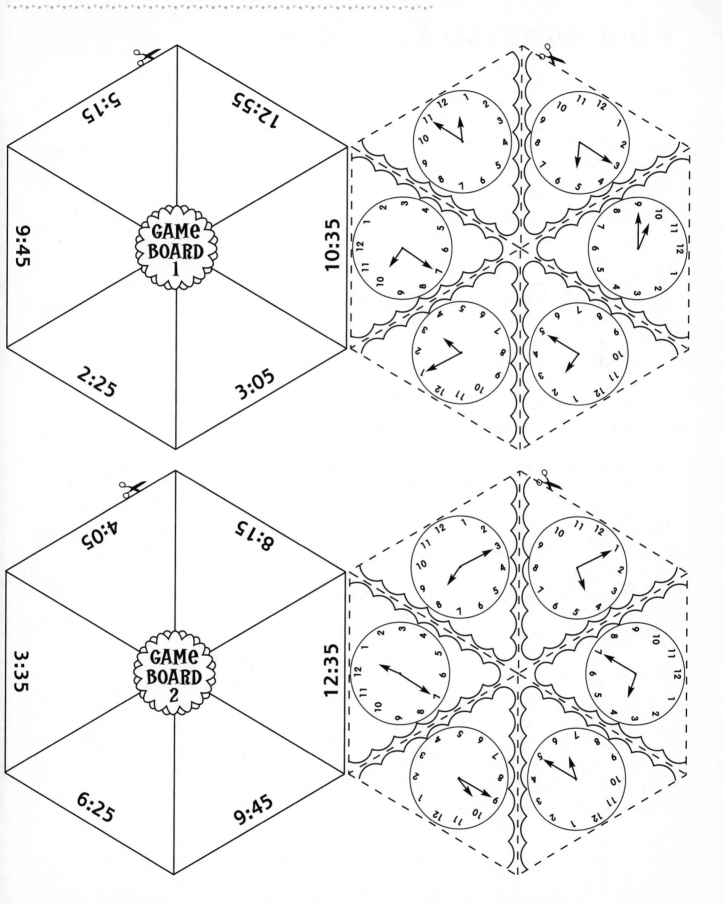

Clock-ominoes

Materials

• Clock-ominoes game cards (pages 23–24)

How to Play

1. One player shuffles the game cards, passes out six cards to each player, and places one card faceup on the table. Then the player places each of the remaining cards facedown on the table.

2. The first player checks to see if any of his or her cards shows a clock that matches one of the times shown on the card on the table.

> ✳ If the player finds a match, he or she places that end of the card next to the matching end of the card on the table. Then the turn ends.

> ✳ If the player does not have a match, he or she selects one of the cards turned facedown on the table. If that card has a matching clock, the player plays the card on the table and the turn ends. If the player cannot make a match, he or she keeps the card and the turn ends.

3. Players continue to take turns. On each turn, a player tries to match a clock on one of his or her cards to a clock shown on the table. The first player to use all of his or her cards wins the game.

Variation

Have players place all the cards facedown on the table. Then players take turns tossing a penny to determine how many cards to select: one if the penny lands heads up, and two if it lands tails up. The player looks at one card at a time, reads the time on the clocks, and tells how much time difference there is between the two clocks. If the player answers correctly, he or she keeps the card. If incorrect, the player returns the card facedown to the table.

Answer Key
Players should agree whether or not answers are correct.

Clock-ominoes Game Cards

5:30	7:05	2:55	10:45	4:50
3:35	6:10	11:25	12:30	9:45
2:20	8:15	1:30	7:55	5:40

Clock-ominoes Game Cards

| 12:15 | 3:55 | 9:10 | 1:00 | 3:25 |

| 10:15 | 2:05 | 7:45 | 4:20 | 8:25 |

| 5:50 | 11:40 | 3:00 | 6:35 | 9:20 |

Clocking In

Materials

- Clocking In game board (page 26)
- Clocking In game cards (pages 27–28)
- Game Clock pattern (page 16)
- Brass fastener (for clock)
- Number cube (page 48)
- 1 button per player, each a different color (for game markers)

How to Play

1. One player shuffles the game cards and places the stack facedown on the table. Each player places a game marker on START.

2. The first player turns over the top card in the stack, reads the problem, and tells the answer. The player may use the game clock to help him or her arrive at the answer.

* If the answer is correct, the player rolls the number cube and moves that number of spaces clockwise around the outer circle of the clock. If the player lands on a "Clock In!" space, he or she moves in to the next circle.

* If the player's answer is incorrect, the turn ends and he or she places the card on the bottom of the stack.

3. Players continue to take turns. Each time a player lands on a "Clock In!" space, he or she moves in to the next circle. Then the player moves around that circle until he or she lands on another "Clock In!" space. (If a player moves around the outer circle more than once, he or she treats START as one space.) The first player to reach FINISH at the center of the clock wins the game.

Variation

Write each answer (see Answer Key) on a separate index card and its item number on the back. Place the game cards faceup on one end of the table and the answers faceup on the other end. Then invite two teams of five players each to hold a relay. On a signal, one player on each team takes a game card, solves the problem, finds the card with his or her answer, and then checks the back of the card to see if the item number of the answer matches the number of the problem. If correct, the player keeps the cards and the next player on his or her team takes a turn. If incorrect, the player returns each card faceup on its end of the table and the next player takes a turn. The team with the most cards at the end of the game wins.

OBJECTIVE

To correctly solve word problems about time and be the first player to move his or her game marker to FINISH

PLAYERS: 2-3

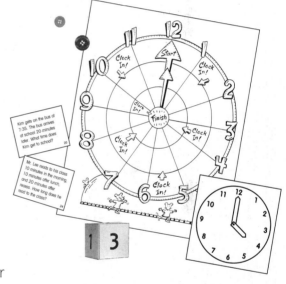

Answer Key

1. 11:00	16. 45 minutes
2. 1:35	17. 4:50
3. 45 minutes	18. 3:35
4. 10:35	19. 6:35
5. 10:15	20. 7:55
6. 1:20	21. Ray's art class is 15 minutes longer.
7. 7:55	
8. 4 hours 15 minutes	22. 1 hour 20 minutes
9. 45 minutes	23. 35 minutes
10. 8:50	24. 40 minutes
11. 15 minutes	25. 35 minutes
12. 25 minutes	26. 4:15
13. 10:05	27. 50 minutes
14. Afternoon recess is 5 minutes longer.	28. 7:50
	29. 35 minutes
15. 30 minutes	30. 5:05

25

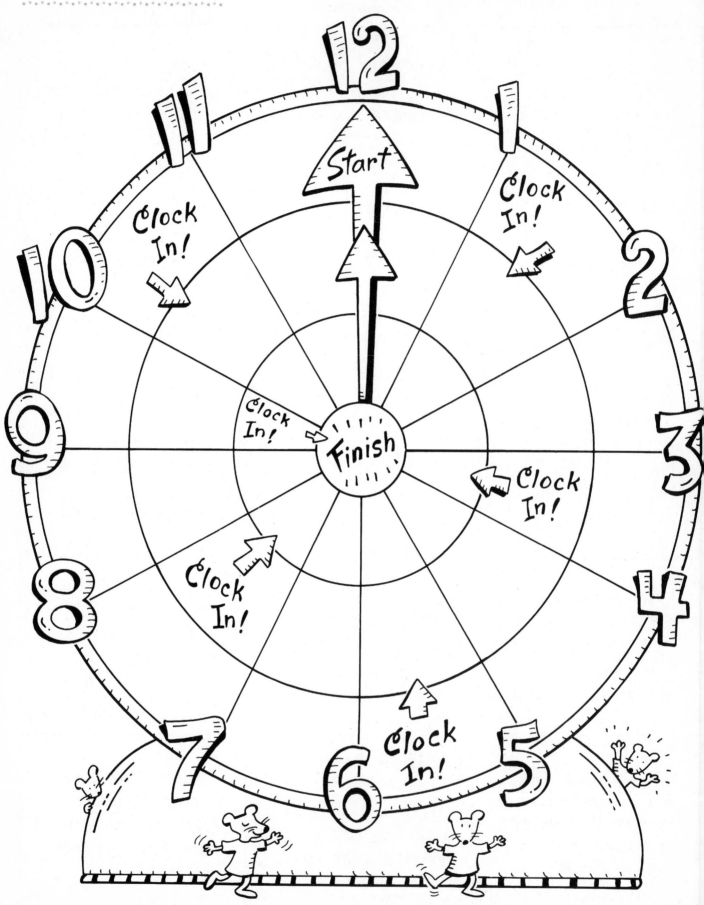

Zoe's school starts at 8:00. Her art class begins three hours later. What time does Zoe go to Art? **1**	Ana spends 25 minutes in Music every day. Music begins at 1:10. What time does Music end? **2**	Juan goes to lunch at 11:30. His lunch ends at 12:15. How much time does Juan have to eat lunch? **3**
Pat went to the library at 10:15. She stayed for 20 minutes. What time did Pat return to class? **4**	Han's reading class begins at 9:00 and lasts for 1 hour and 15 minutes. What time does Reading end? **5**	Cami worked on her science project for 10 minutes. She stopped at 1:30. What time did Cami begin? **6**
Bus 123 gets to school at 7:40. Today it was 15 minutes late. What time did Bus 123 arrive? **7**	Mr. Jones's class left for a field trip at 9:05. The class returned at 1:20. How long did the field trip last? **8**	The class hamster in Room 15 took a nap from 10:20 until 11:05. How long did the hamster sleep? **9**
Miss Perez's class started silent reading at 8:35. The class read for 15 minutes. What time did they stop reading? **10**	Karl spends 40 minutes in the computer lab and 55 minutes in Math. How much more time does he spend in Math? **11**	Liz did her spelling homework in 10 minutes and math in 15 minutes. How much time did she spend on homework? **12**
Ivan started his spelling test at 9:45. He spent 20 minutes on the test. What time did Ivan finish? **13**	Nita has morning recess from 10:00 to 10:15. Her afternoon recess lasts from 12:40 to 1:00. Which recess is longer? **14**	Joel read three books in class. He spent 10 minutes on each book. How long did Joel read? **15**

Clocking In Game Cards

Jess read 20 minutes in class, 10 minutes on the bus, and 15 minutes at home. How much time did Jess spend reading?

16

Ben arrives at his after-school program at 3:15. He stays 1 hour and 35 minutes. What time does Ben leave?

17

Meg called Sal 45 minutes after she got home from school. They started talking at 4:20. What time did Meg get home?

18

Eric usually wakes up at 6:15 to get ready for school. Today he slept 20 minutes longer. What time did Eric wake up?

19

Kim gets on the bus at 7:35. The bus arrives at school 20 minutes later. What time does Kim get to school?

20

Ray's P.E. class lasts for 35 minutes. His art class begins at 12:50 and ends at 1:40. Which class is longer?

21

The school cook starts making lunch at 10:30. The food is ready to serve at 11:50. How long does it take the cook to make lunch?

22

Mrs. Sims's P.E. class ran for 10 minutes, played soccer for 20 minutes, and rested for 5 minutes. How long did the class last?

23

Mr. Lee reads to his class 10 minutes in the morning, 10 minutes after lunch, and 20 minutes after recess. How long does he read to the class?

24

Todd walked his dog after school. He left at 3:35 and returned at 4:10. How long did Todd walk his dog?

25

Yuri played for 45 minutes before doing his homework. He started playing at 3:30. What time did Yuri start his homework?

26

Abby leaves for school at 7:20. She wakes up at 6:30. How much time does she have to get ready for school?

27

Bob walks 10 minutes to school each day. School starts at 8:00. What time does he need to leave to get to school on time?

28

After school Lim raked leaves for 20 minutes and pulled weeds for 15 minutes. How long did Lim work?

29

Jen started her homework at 4:10. She read for 35 minutes and studied spelling for 20 minutes. What time did she finish?

30

Ka-ching!

Materials

• Ka-ching! game cards (pages 30–31)

How to Play

1. One player shuffles the cards and deals them evenly between the two players. Each player places his or her stack of cards facedown on the table.

2. Each player turns over the top card on his or her stack and finds the value for the coin combination on the card. Players announce their answers. Then the player with the higher coin value says "Ka-ching!" to indicate that he or she wins the round. That player collects the cards and sets them aside.

* If the coin values are "tied," or the same, each player turns over another card and announces the coin value on the new card. The player with the higher coin value breaks the tie and takes all the cards in play.

3. Play continues until all the cards have been used. The player with the most cards at the end of the game wins.

Variation

Instead of turning over one card at a time, challenge players to turn over two cards. Then have each player add the value of the coin combinations on both of his or her cards. The player with the higher value wins the round.

Answer Key			
1. 2¢	11. 36¢	21. 37¢	31. 75¢
2. 6¢	12. 30¢	22. 50¢	32. 75¢
3. 8¢	13. 28¢	23. 15¢	33. 31¢
4. 30¢	14. 45¢	24. 30¢	34. 31¢
5. 15¢	15. 40¢	25. 12¢	35. 11¢
6. 20¢	16. 32¢	26. 35¢	36. 21¢
7. 26¢	17. 55¢	27. 20¢	37. 21¢
8. 16¢	18. 36¢	28. 30¢	38. 17¢
9. 31¢	19. 22¢	29. 50¢	39. 14¢
10. 35¢	20. 27¢	30. 22¢	40. 40¢

Ka-ching! Game Cards

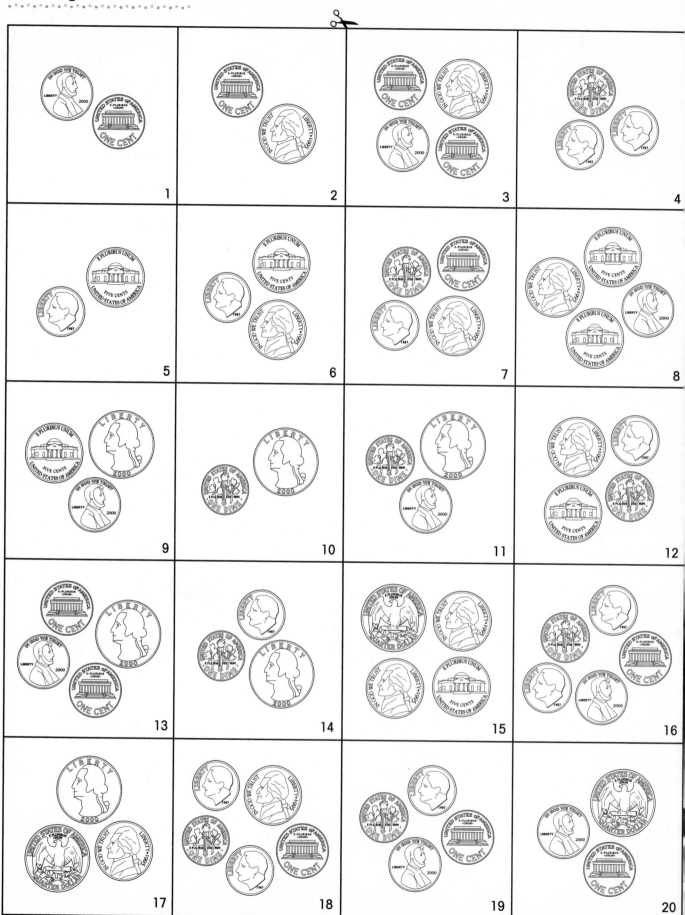

Math Games to Master Basic Skills: Time & Money   Scholastic Teaching Resources

Piggy Bank Play-Off

Materials

- Laminated Piggy Bank Play-Off game board (page 33)
- Piggy Bank Play-Off number spinner (page 34)
- Piggy Bank Play-Off coin spinner (page 34)
- 2 sets of penny, nickel, dime, and quarter coin cards (page 47)
- 2 wipe-off crayons or markers
- Paper towels

How to Play

1. Players place all the coins faceup on the table near the game board.

2. The first player spins the number spinner. Then the player spins the coin spinner that number of times. After each spin, the player takes a coin that matches the coin on the spinner. Once all the coins are collected for his or her turn, the player adds the value of the coins together.

 ✳ If the player names the correct value, he or she draws an X on any space on the game board. Then the player returns the coins faceup to the table.

 ✳ If the player names an incorrect value, the turn ends. The player returns the coins faceup to the table.

3. The second player takes his or her turn. If the player names the correct value for the coins collected, he or she draws an O on any blank space on the game board.

4. Players continue to take turns. Each time a correct value is named for the collected coins, the player draws his or her mark in a blank space on the game board. The first player to mark three spaces in a row wins the game. (If all the spaces are filled and no player has three symbols in a row, the game is a tie and there is no winner.)

Variation

Add two more sets of coin cards to increase the difficulty of the game. To play, a player spins the number spinner and the coin spinner, and then takes that number of the coin that the spinner lands on. After doing this three times, the player finds the total value of all of his or her coins. If correct, the player draws his or her mark on the game board.

Answer Key

Answers will vary according to the number and type of coins the spinner lands on. Players should agree whether or not answers are correct.

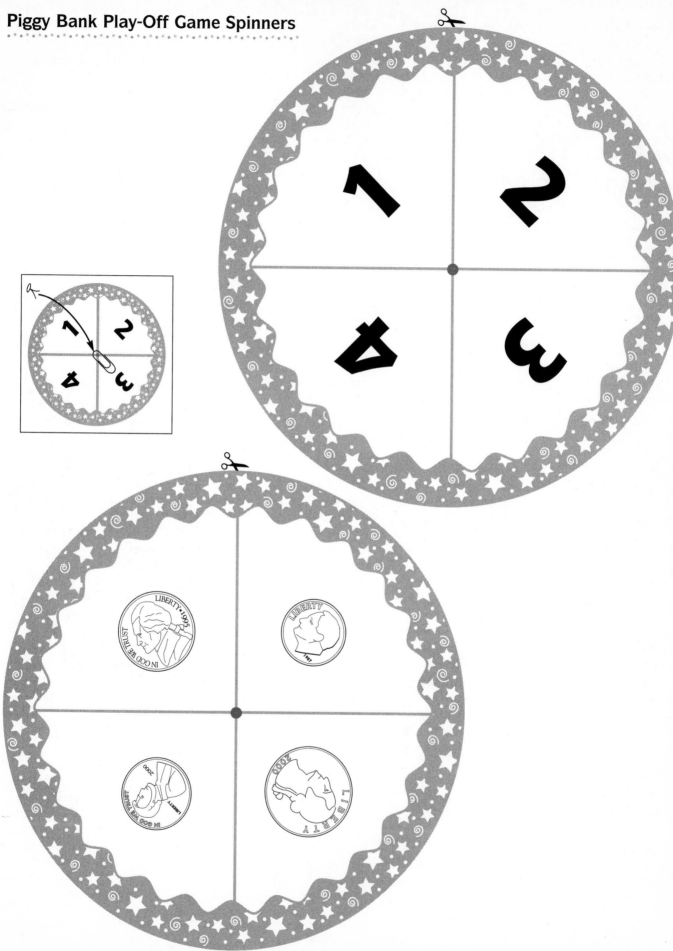

Math Games to Master Basic Skills: Time & Money Scholastic Teaching Resources

Gold Rush!

Materials

- Gold Rush! game board (page 36)
- Penny, nickel, dime, quarter, and half-dollar coin cards (page 47)
- Operations cube (page 48)
- Small paper bag
- 1 button per player, each a different color (for game markers)

How to Play

1. One player puts the coin cards in the paper bag. Each player places a game marker on START.

2. The first player draws two coin cards from the bag. Then he or she rolls the cube. If the cube lands on a +, the player adds the two coins to find the sum of their values. If it lands on a −, the player subtracts the lower coin value from the higher coin value to find the difference.

 ✳ If the player answers correctly, he or she moves the number of spaces shown on the cube and follows any directions shown on the space. Then the player returns the coins to the bag.

 ✳ If the player's answer is incorrect, he or she does not move and the turn ends. At the end of his or her turn, the player returns the coin cards to the bag.

3. Players continue to take turns. The first player to reach FINISH at the cart of gold wins the game.

Variation

To increase the difficulty of the game, invite each player to draw two coins from the bag twice, keeping the two sets separate. After the player rolls the cube, have him or her add or subtract the two sets of coins, depending on the operation rolled on the cube.

Answer Key
Answers will vary according to the operation rolled on the cube and the value of the coin cards pulled from the bag. Players should agree whether or not answers are correct.

Gold Rush! Game Board

Start

Go back 1 space.

Skip next turn.

Go ahead 2 spaces.

Go back 2 spaces.

Take another turn.

Go ahead 1 space.

Finish

Math Games to Master Basic Skills: Time & Money Scholastic Teaching Resources

Off to the Bank · · · · · · · · · ·

Materials

- Off to the Bank game board (page 38)
- 1 set of coin cards per player (page 47)
- Number cube pattern (page 48)
- 1 button per player, each a different color (for game markers)

How to Play

1. Each player takes a set of coin cards (5 pennies, 4 nickels, 3 dimes, 2 quarters, and 2 half-dollars). Then he or she places a game marker on the money bag.

2. The first player rolls the number cube and moves his or her marker that number of spaces. The player follows the directions on the space. If the space shows a money amount, the player puts together any combination of his or her coin cards to equal that value.

  ✳ If the coin combination equals the value shown on the space, the player leaves his or her marker on the space and the turn ends.

  ✳ If the coin combination does not equal the amount on the space, the player moves his or her marker back the number of spaces shown on the cube and the turn ends.

3. Players continue to take turns, moving around the board as many times as needed to complete the game. (Each player keeps his or her own coin cards after each turn.) When a player comes to one of the short paths to the BANK, he or she decides whether or not to follow that path or continue on the main path. To reach the BANK, players must roll the exact number of spaces on the number cube. The first player to reach the BANK wins the game.

Variation

To reinforce adding and subtracting money values, use the operations cube (page 48) and an additional set of coin cards. Place these cards facedown near the game board and mix them up. To play, a player picks one of the cards, rolls the cube, and moves that number of spaces. Then the player adds or subtracts the value on the space and the value of the coin card, using his or her own set of coin cards to find the answer if needed. When the turn ends, the player returns the one coin card facedown to the playing area.

OBJECTIVE

To make coin combinations that equal a given value and be the first player to move his or her marker to the BANK

PLAYERS: 2–4

Answer Key

Answers will vary according to the coin combinations that players use to equal each value on the game board. Players should agree whether or not answers are correct.

Off to the Bank Game Board

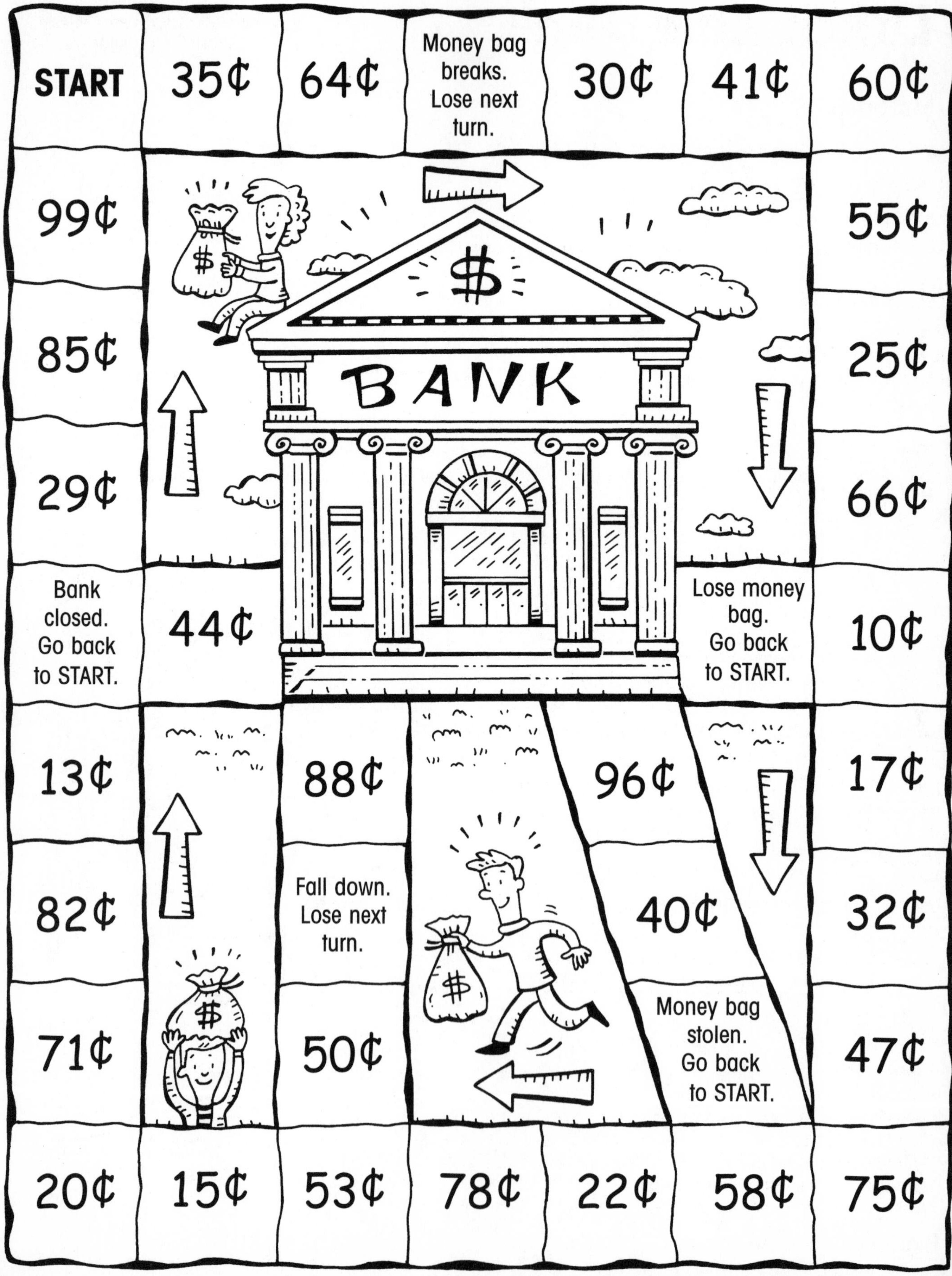

| START | 35¢ | 64¢ | Money bag breaks. Lose next turn. | 30¢ | 41¢ | 60¢ |

99¢

85¢

29¢

Bank closed. Go back to START.

44¢

55¢

25¢

66¢

Lose money bag. Go back to START.

10¢

BANK

13¢

82¢

71¢

88¢

Fall down. Lose next turn.

50¢

96¢

40¢

Money bag stolen. Go back to START.

17¢

32¢

47¢

| 20¢ | 15¢ | 53¢ | 78¢ | 22¢ | 58¢ | 75¢ |

Math Games to Master Basic Skills: Time & Money Scholastic Teaching Resources

Lunch Line

Materials

- Lunch Line game board (page 40)
- Lunch Line menu cards (pages 41–42)
- Number cube (page 48)
- 1 button per player, each a different color (for game markers)

How to Play

1. One player shuffles the menu cards and places the stack facedown near the game board. Each player places a marker on START.

2. The first player turns over the top card in the stack. He or she reads the menu, adds the menu items together, and tells the answer.

* If correct, the player rolls the number cube and moves that many spaces. He or she follows the directions on the space and then the turn ends.

* If incorrect, the player does not roll the cube and the turn ends.

3. Players continue to take turns. At the end of each player's turn, he or she puts the menu card on the bottom of the stack. The first player to reach "Paid!" and move to the table wins the game.

Variation

After a player correctly adds the cost of the items on his or her menu card, have the player find the difference in cost between the highest- and lowest-priced items. If he or she answers correctly, the player rolls the cube again and moves that number of spaces.

OBJECTIVE

To add the price of foods on the menu cards and be the first player to go through the lunch line and move to the table

PLAYERS: 2-3

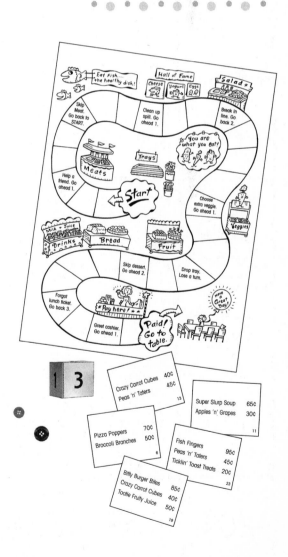

Answer Key				
1. $1.30	7. $1.40	13. 85¢	19. $1.75	25. $1.75
2. $1.10	8. $1.30	14. 65¢	20. $1.50	26. $1.20
3. $1.45	9. $1.10	15. 50¢	21. $1.45	27. $1.95
4. $1.25	10. $1.10	16. $1.75	22. $1.50	28. $1.50
5. $1.30	11. 95¢	17. $1.35	23. $1.60	29. $1.40
6. $1.20	12. $1.00	18. $1.80	24. $1.35	30. $1.75

Lunch Line Game Board

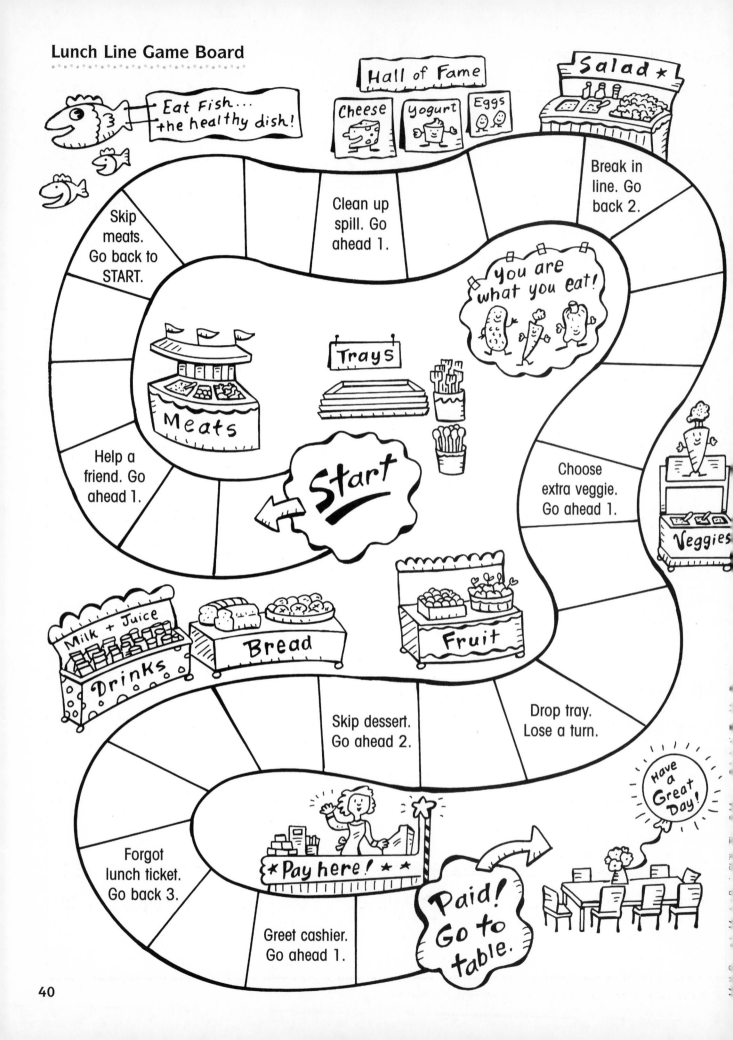

Eat Fish... the healthy dish!

Hall of Fame

Cheese

Yogurt

Eggs

Salad ★

Skip meats. Go back to START.

Clean up spill. Go ahead 1.

Break in line. Go back 2.

You are what you eat!

Help a friend. Go ahead 1.

Meats

Trays

Start

Choose extra veggie. Go ahead 1.

Veggies

Drinks

Milk + Juice

Bread

Fruit

Drop tray. Lose a turn.

Skip dessert. Go ahead 2.

Have a Great Day!

Forgot lunch ticket. Go back 3.

★ Pay here! ★ ★

Paid! Go to table.

Greet cashier. Go ahead 1.

Lunch Line Menu Cards

Cheesy Ham Strips 80¢ Fresh-Baked Fries 50¢ **1**	Tuna Tasties 75¢ Banana Blast 35¢ **2**	Cha-cha Chili 90¢ Peach-Pear Punch 55¢ **3**
Bitty Burger Bites 85¢ Salad Delight 40¢ **4**	Chicken Niblets 95¢ Really Rockin' Rice 35¢ **5**	Pizza Poppers 70¢ Broccoli Branches 50¢ **6**
Beefaroni Bake 80¢ Veggie Volcano 60¢ **7**	Fish Fingers 95¢ Moo-Good Milk 35¢ **8**	Mini Dippin' Dogs 65¢ Orange Sip-Up 45¢ **9**
Meatloaf Magic 85¢ Watermelon Wings 25¢ **10**	Super Slurp Soup 65¢ Apples 'n' Grapes 30¢ **11**	Corn Kabobs 55¢ Lean Green Beans 45¢ **12**
Crazy Carrot Cubes 40¢ Peas 'n' Taters 45¢ **13**	Bagel Boosters 15¢ Tootie Fruity Juice 50¢ **14**	Fruit Fritter 20¢ So-Yummy Yogurt 30¢ **15**

Cheesy Ham Strips 80¢ Veggie Volcano 60¢ Moo-Good Milk 35¢ 16	Cha-cha Chili 90¢ Apples 'n' Grapes 30¢ Bagel Boosters 15¢ 17	Tuna Tasties 75¢ Corn Kabobs 55¢ Broccoli Branches 50¢ 18
Bitty Burger Bites 85¢ Crazy Carrot Cubes 40¢ Tootie Fruity Juice 50¢ 19	Chicken Niblets 95¢ Salad Delight 40¢ Baked Bread Bones 15¢ 20	Pizza Poppers 70¢ Lean Green Beans 45¢ So-Yummy Yogurt 30¢ 21
Beefaroni Bake 80¢ Watermelon Wings 25¢ Orange Sip-Up 45¢ 22	Fish Fingers 95¢ Peas 'n' Taters 45¢ Ticklin' Toast Treats 20¢ 23	Mini Dippin' Dogs 65¢ Fresh-Baked Fries 50¢ Fruit Fritter 20¢ 24
Meatloaf Magic 85¢ Really Rockin' Rice 35¢ Peach-Pear Punch 55¢ 25	Super Slurp Soup 65¢ Salad Delight 40¢ Baked Bread Bones 15¢ 26	Bitty Burger Bites 85¢ Corn Kabobs 55¢ Peach-Pear Punch 55¢ 27
Tuna Tasties 75¢ Crazy Carrot Cubes 40¢ Moo-Good Milk 35¢ 28	Pizza Poppers 70¢ Peas 'n' Taters 45¢ Watermelon Wings 25¢ 29	Beefaroni Bake 80¢ Lean Green Beans 45¢ Tootie Fruity Juice 50¢ 30

Math Games to Master Basic Skills: Time & Money Scholastic Teaching Resources

Money Roll

Materials

- Money Roll game board (page 44)
- Paper money cards, 1 set per player and 10 sets for the game board (page 47)
- Paper money cube (page 48)
- Number cube (page 48)
- 1 button per player, each a different color (for game markers)

How to Play

1. One player stacks the 20 paper money cards for each denomination on the matching box on the game board. Then each player takes his or her set of paper money cards (two $1, two $5, two $10, and two $20) and places a marker on START.

2. The first player rolls the paper money cube. He or she takes that amount of money from the money boxes on the game board. Then the player rolls the number cube and moves that number of spaces. He or she follows the directions on the space.

* If the player must pay money, he or she places that amount in the boxes on the game board.

* If the player is directed to take money, he or she takes that amount from the game board.

3. Players continue to take turns. When a player lands on or passes the "Payday!" space, he or she takes $75 from the game board. After all the players reach FINISH, they count their money. The player with the most money at the end of the game wins. (If a player runs out of money before reaching FINISH, he or she is out of the game.)

Variation

Use only the paper money cards and the two cubes for this variation. To play, each player rolls the paper money cube. Then he or she rolls the number cube to see how many paper money cards to take. The player rolls both cubes again and puts the new set of paper money cards with his or her first set. After every player takes a turn, they find the value of all their paper money cards. The player with the highest value wins the round and collects all the cards. Play continues until all the money has been used. The player with the most money at the end of the game wins.

OBJECTIVE

To make combinations with paper money that equal a given value and be the player with the most money at the end of the game

PLAYERS: 2-3

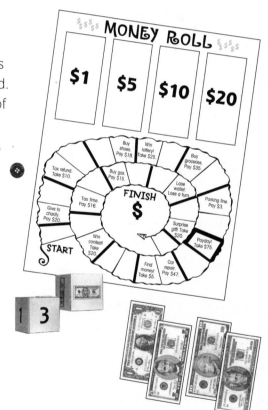

Answer Key

Players should check each other's work and agree whether or not they counted out the correct amount for each money value rolled, paid, or collected.

MONEY ROLL

$1 $5 $10 $20

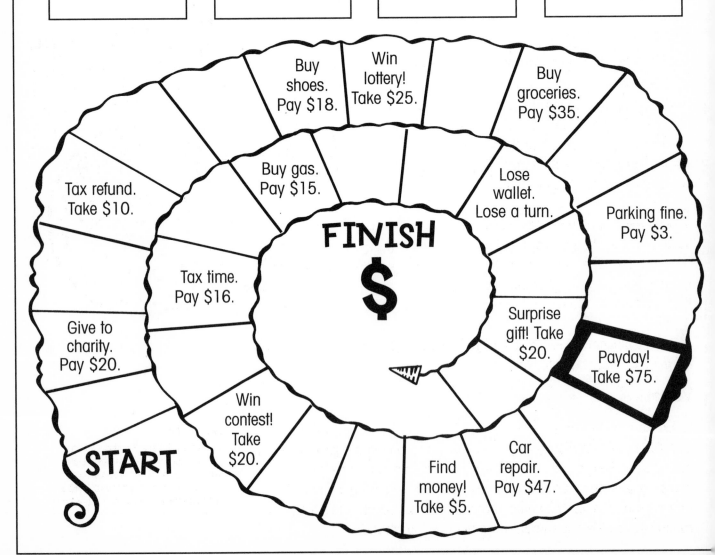

Buy shoes. Pay $18.

Win lottery! Take $25.

Buy groceries. Pay $35.

Tax refund. Take $10.

Buy gas. Pay $15.

Lose wallet. Lose a turn.

Parking fine. Pay $3.

Tax time. Pay $16.

FINISH $

Give to charity. Pay $20.

Surprise gift! Take $20.

Payday! Take $75.

Win contest! Take $20.

START

Find money! Take $5.

Car repair. Pay $47.

Shopping Spree •••••••••••

Materials

- Laminated Shopping Spree game card for each player (page 46)
- Shopping Spree game spinner (page 46)
- Brass fastener (for spinner)
- Paper clip (for spinner)
- Wipe-off crayon or marker for each player
- Paper towels

How to Play

1. Each player selects a game card and wipe-off crayon or marker.

2. The first player spins the spinner and names the price of the item it lands on. He or she writes the price under the money bag in number 1 on his or her game card. The player subtracts to solve the problem and writes the answer on the bottom line.

 * If correct, the player writes that amount on the money bag in number 2.

 * If the answer is incorrect, the player erases the answer and solves the problem again. The player works the problem until he or she finds the correct answer (other players may help him or her on the third try). Then he or she writes that amount on the money bag in number 2 and the turn ends.

3. Players continue to take turns. On each turn, the player spins the spinner, writes the price of the item under the money bag, subtracts to solve the problem, and then writes the answer on the bottom line and on the next money bag. After players complete number 4, they compare their final answers. The player with the highest amount of money wins the round.

4. To play another round, players erase their game cards with paper towels. The first player to win three rounds wins the game.

Variation

To provide practice in subtracting with higher amounts, mask the $25.00 in the first money bag. Then copy and laminate a game card for each player. Before play, players write a given amount in the first money bag (such as $43.50) and use this as the starting amount for that round. Keep the game interesting by having players start each round with a different amount from the previous round.

OBJECTIVE

To write and solve subtraction problems involving money and be the first player to win three rounds of play

PLAYERS: 2-3

Answer Key

Answers will vary. Players should check each other's work and agree whether or not their answers are correct. (Players might want to use a calculator to check their answers.)

Shopping Spree Game Card and Spinner

SHOPPING SPREE

1	2	3	4
$ $\underline{25}$. $\underline{00}$	$ ___ . ___	$ ___ . ___	$ ___ . ___
-$ ___ . ___	-$ ___ . ___	-$ ___ . ___	-$ ___ . ___
$ ___ . ___	$ ___ . ___	$ ___ . ___	$ ___ . ___

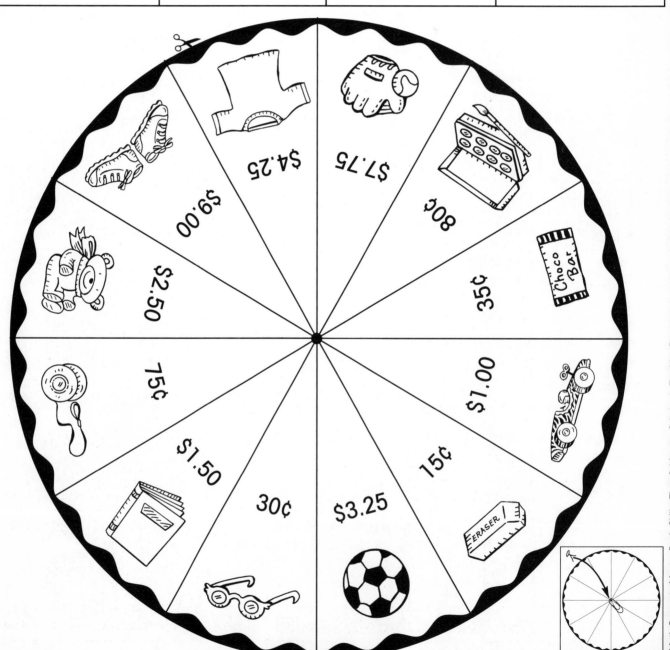

$4.25 $7.75   80¢ $9.00   35¢ $2.50 $1.00   75¢   15¢ $1.50   30¢ $3.25

Coin and Paper Money Cards

Game Cubes

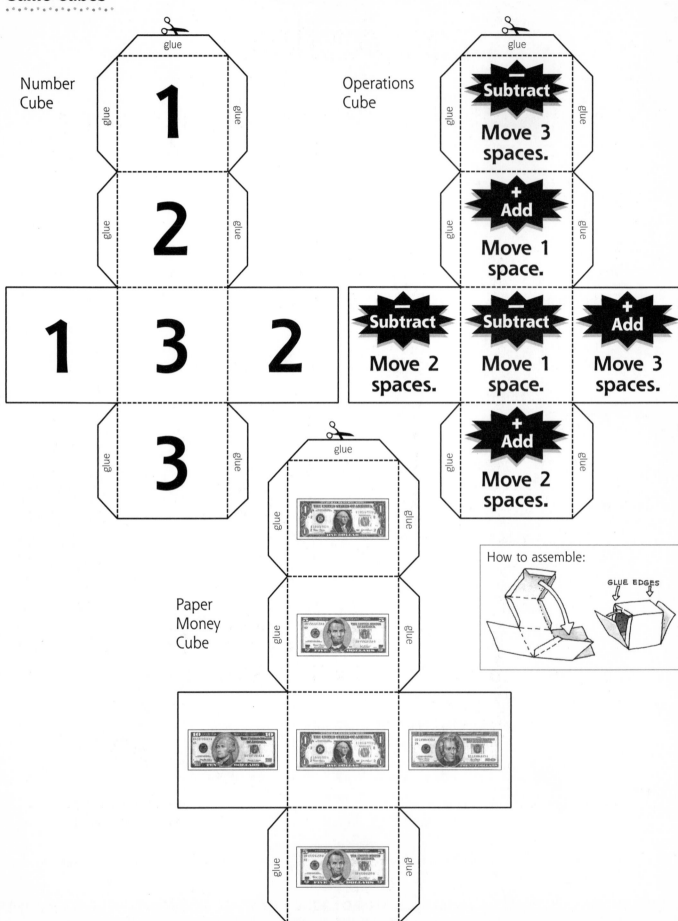

Number Cube

Operations Cube

Paper Money Cube

How to assemble:

GLUE EDGES

Math Games to Master Basic Skills: Time & Money Scholastic Teaching Resources